Wasps

Addison-Wesley Publishers Limited
London - Reading, Massachusetts
Menlo Park, California
Amsterdam - Don Mills, Ontario - Sydney
Singapore - Manila - Tokyo

Books in this series
1 Social insects
2 Bees
3 Ants
4 Wasps

Original edition © 1982 Munksgaard International Publishers Ltd, Copenhagen.
This edition © 1982 Addison-Wesley Publishers Ltd, 53 Bedford Square, London WC1B 3DZ.
Philippines copyright 1982 by Addison-Wesley Publishers Ltd.
ISBN 0 201 14352 6

Acknowledgements
The publishers wish to thank the following for their kind permission to reproduce photographs:
Hansen, Elvig: 1, 4, 5, 6(2), 7, 8, 9, 10, 11, 12, 13, 14, 15, 16, 17, 18, 19, 20, 21 below, 24, 29
Hansen, Gerth: 28 top
Schmidt, Ulla: 28 bottom, 30
Westergaard Knudsen, Niels: 21 top, 23, 25, 26, 27, 31, cover

Danish author: Pia Korsholm
Drawings: Bjarne Nielsen

Printed by Europrinte, Portugal

Contents

In a cake shop on a hot summer's day you may see black and yellow striped insects, especially on the cakes. These insects look like bees. On closer inspection you will discover that most of these insects are *not* bees. They are wasps. Most people do not like wasps because their stings are very painful.

Some wasps live in colonies just like honeybees. These social wasps will be described in this book. The easiest way to distinguish a wasp from a honeybee is that a wasp is less hairy. The wasp does not live on pollen like the honeybee. (You can read more about this in the book *Bees* in this series.) Other ways of distinguishing wasps from bees are: 1) Wasps' wings are folded along the top of their bodies when resting. 2) Their compound eyes have an indentation in front. 3) Their jaws are more firmly developed, and their tongues are shorter than the bees. The structure of a wasp's mouth is not the same as a honeybee's. This indicates that the wasp eats different types of food.

A wasp emerging from its pupa. The strong jaws and bent antennae can be clearly seen.

The adult wasp lives on dissolved sugar substances. Its narrow gullet prevents it from eating solid food. Generally wasps get their sugar by collecting nectar from flowers. The wasp's tongue is short. It can only collect from flowers where it can easily reach the nectar. Wasps also collect honeydew from greenfly. (You can read more about this in the book *Ants* in this series.) Sometimes wasps invade a beehive and steal the honey from the bees' store. Wasps will eat any sweet things they meet from the juice of apples, still hanging on the tree, to jam and icing on cakes.

Wasps prey on other insects. The wasp kills by biting the insect's head off with its strong jaws. It does not often use its sting on the victim. The wasp does not live on these insects. Instead it chews them up and feeds them to its larvae. In this way the larvae get protein which is necessary for them to develop normally. Wasps also eat meat which is not covered up in a butcher's or in a kitchen.

Newly-hatched queen being fed by workers.

Two wasps and a honeybee (above) suck the juice from an overripe plum.

The larvae are fed with both fluid and more solid food. The adult wasp regurgitates it from its crop. This is the equivalent of the honeybee's honeysac. When a larva has been given food, it produces a drop from saliva glands in its head. The drop is eaten by the adult. These drops are necessary for all wasps. If, for example, you removed all the larvae, the colony would break up. The queen would die. The workers would desert the nest.

An exchange of food also takes place between the workers. This happens in a very special way. The worker which wants food touches another wasp's mouth with its antennae. The touched wasp then regurgitates a drop of food.

A wasp has caught a house fly and is cutting it into pieces.

All wasp colonies in Europe are annual. The fertilised queen hibernates during winter. In April or May the queen comes out of hibernation. She begins to search for food and starts to build a nest. Where the nest is built depends on what kind of wasp it is and what suitable place the queen can find.

Some wasps build underground nests, for example in a deserted mole's nest. Others build nests in attics. Wasps also build their nests in empty trees, in birdhouses and hanging on bushes. Wasps use dead wood to build their nests. The wood is chewed with saliva. This forms a sort of paper pulp. The nest is built from this pulp, which gives it a grey or brown colour.

The queen begins to build the nest by collecting some pulp under the chosen spot. The pulp is formed into a vertical sheet with a little stem. Two small cells, shaped like inverted bowls, are attached to the stem. The cells are open at the bottom. Above and around these cells, a mantle is built out from the stem (1). The mantle looks like an umbrella. It must protect the eggs and the larvae. More cells are built around the first two, and a sort of comb is made (2). Wasp combs are horizontal, while

Queen gnawing a piece of wood. She takes the chewed wood back to the nest.

1

2

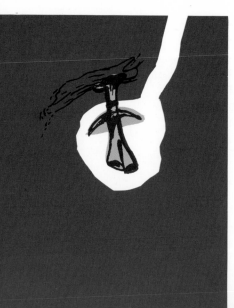

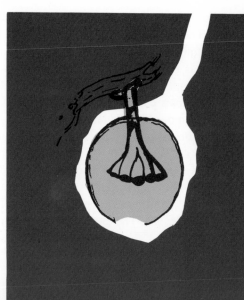

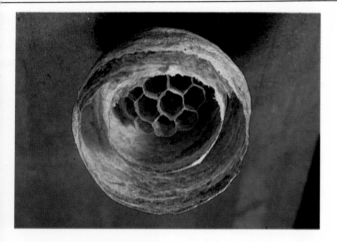

The start of a wasps' nest. The queen has built the first combs with two mantles around them.

most bee combs are vertical. As the number of cells is increased, more mantles are built around them (3). The distance between the mantles is about half the width of the queen's body (about 2.5 mm). When the queen builds, she holds on to the edge of the new mantle with her second and third pair of legs. She uses her forelegs and jaws to build the new mantle.

Building a wasps' nest underground. 1, 2 and 3: look in the text. 4, the finished nest.

3

4

It takes the queen quite a long time to build all this. She is constantly flying back and forth between the nest and the spot where she collects the building material. Once in a while she has to rest. She has a particular place in the nest for resting. This is between the bottom of the first cells and the place where the first mantle is attached. There is just enough room for her when she wraps herself around the stem.

In three days the queen will have built between five and nine cells. She lays eggs in the cells as soon as they are made. The eggs are fastened to the bottom of the cell. The queen collects pulp until the eggs begin to hatch. Within five or six days the first larvae start to emerge. The queen starts collecting food for them. At the same time she continues to expand the nest.

Between 20 and 40 cells are built before the first adult wasps appear. These are workers and cannot lay eggs. The amount of time it takes for the adults to appear varies greatly. It depends, among other things, on the type of wasp and weather conditions. The better the weather, the faster they emerge. But it always takes at least three weeks and often four or more. From the middle of June the queen does not leave the nest.

The workers have now taken over most of the queen's duties. Her only duty now is to lay eggs. In some types of wasp, the queen can lay between 20 000 and 25 000 eggs during the summer.

The queen lays one egg in each cell. The eggs are 1 mm in length, white and sausage-shaped. The larvae emerge after about five days. They produce a sticky substance which binds them to the cell. This means they cannot fall out of their cells, which are open. The larvae are fed by the workers. As the larvae grow, they shed their skins. They do this five times in all.

The largest larvae make a scraping sound with their jaws on the side of the cell when they are hungry. The workers can hear this sound and one of them approaches the larva. It touches the larva with its jaws and deposits a drop of food. The larva produces a drop of saliva which the worker licks up (see page 7). The larva then eats the drop of food. The portion of the food, which the larva cannot digest, builds up as a black mass in the intestines.

After 15 days the larva has become so large that it fills the whole cell. It stops eating and begins to pupate. It spins a cocoon of fine silk thread around itself. These threads are formed in the larva's saliva glands. When the cocoon is finished, the larva drops its excrement. The change to an adult insect can now begin.

After 10—15 days the adult wasp is fully developed. It tears open the cocoon with its jaws and crawls out of its cell.

Portion of comb with a larva and pupae at various stages. The larva and youngest pupae are on the left. D.

egg | larva | | pupa | adult wasp

Workers feeding larvae.

Like honeybees, wasps carry out various duties, according to their age. Unlike honeybees they do not stick strictly to this rule. A wasp can, in the course of a day, work both inside and outside the nest.

The newly hatched wasp is soft and vulnerable. Therefore it stays in the nest. It lives partially on the food received from other workers, and partially on the substance that the larvae produce. When its skin hardens it can begin to work.

The wasp's first duties are performed inside the nest. It feeds the young with food brought home by older hunting wasps. It cleans the cells as well, getting rid of old cocoons and other debris. It also helps to rebuild the nest.

After a few days, the wasp is ready to begin its outdoor work. But first it must fly around near the nest for a while. The wasp learns to recognise the surroundings within a radius of about 9 metres. When it is farther away it senses its direction by the sun, and so can find its way back to the nest. The youngest wasps collect wood. This is scraped from old fenceposts and similar dead wood with their jaws. When the wasps return to the nest the wood is chewed with saliva. This produces the pulp, which is used to build the nest.

Workers cleaning the empty cells.
The white, closed cells still contain pupae.

When the wasps get older, they begin to hunt. They hunt individually, and the prey is usually other insects. Using their strong jaws, they kill the prey, and clip off its wings and legs. This makes it easier to carry the victim to a place where it can be chewed before being taken back to the nest. Wasps also hunt other small animals, alive or dead. Dead moles, mice, or worms are often eaten by wasps.

The older wasps only gather food containing sugar. They make fewer trips than before because it takes longer to collect nectar and other sweet things.

A wasp gathering nectar from a cowparsnip. Note the reddish tongue between its jaws.

When they are more than 30 days old, wasps no longer leave the nest. These older wasps guard the entrance to the nest. If an alien wasp or other enemy tries to get into the nest, the guards use their stings to defend the colony. Wasps from the same nest can recognise one another because they have the same smell.

A worker's life span depends, among other things, on how hard it works. In July, when the work is hardest, a worker's average life span is 14 days. However, the average life span in August is 22 days.

Wasp on guard at entrance to the nest.

When the number of wasps in a colony increases, the nest must expand. This is done by adding cells to the edge of the old comb, and by building new combs. The new combs are built underneath the old ones. Some types of wasps build up to nine combs with more than 20 000 cells. The new combs are attached to the old with thin vertical connectors. To make room for the new combs, the wasps tear down the oldest inner mantles. The paper from these is used, together with new pulp, to build new and larger mantles. Look at the illustration on page 11.

The wasps in a colony collect wood from different places. Therefore the mantles are often striped with many brown and grey colours.

If the nest is underground, the wasps have to dig in order to make the nest bigger. They scrape away the earth with their jaws. The earth is softened with water which the wasps have fetched. In this way they make small balls of earth. The balls can be used to make the entrance the proper size. The wasps remove the remainder by flying away with them. Small stones are carried up to the surface. They can be seen lying around the entrance hole. Larger stones fall to the bottom of the hole. Wasps with nests hanging from branches chew leaves and twigs in order to make more room.

Wasps carrying away pieces of earth from a mouse hole.

Close-up of part of a wasps' nest. The nest is striped because the wasps have collected wood from different places.

Cross-section of an underground wasps' nest.

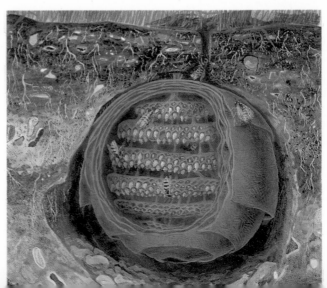

From the middle of July, males and new queens are produced. Males come from unfertilised eggs, which the old queen or perhaps some of the workers have laid. The workers, of course, can lay only unfertilised eggs.

Queens and workers are both female. They develop from fertilised eggs. But queens develop from eggs that are laid in the lowest combs of the nest. They are the last cells to be built. The eggs do not differ from the eggs which become workers. But the larvae in the queen-cells get twice the amount of food that larvae in

The sealed cells contain pupae. The tallest at the back are queen cells.

Males just before swarming.

the smaller cells receive. Consequently they become larger.

The males and the new queens stay in the nest for a while. They live on the nourishing saliva which the larvae produce. They are also fed by the workers. Queens receive more food than the others. Occasionally they fly out to find food for themselves. They store up fat, which they will use during hibernation.

When the males leave the nest at the end of August, they never return. They form swarms which, on warm days, attract the unfertilised queens. This is because of the scent they give off. Queens also attract males with their smell. Upon mating, a queen receives all the sperm necessary for fertilising the eggs for the next year's colony.

All the males die after the mating season. The fertilised queens find a warm place where they can spend the winter, for example under the bark of a tree stump.

Hibernating queen between ceiling boards.

The end of the colony

In September the wasp colony begins to break up. As long as the colony is functioning, the temperature inside the nest stays fairly constant at 30°C. This is possible because the nest's mantle keeps the heat in. The wasps' bodies give off heat. This heat stays in the nest. If it becomes too warm, the wasps cool the air in the nest by rapidly beating their wings, just as honeybees do. If the temperature in the nest becomes very high, the wasps fetch water. They spread out the water on the combs. It evaporates and cools the nest.

As the autumn wears on, the wasps find it difficult to maintain the high temperature in the nest. This is one of the reasons for the disintegration of the colony. The queen and the males use up a lot of the larvae's saliva (see page 7). It is possible that the workers do not get enough. As a result they have less desire to feed the larvae, and many of the larvae die.

When the old queen dies, the workers start fighting among themselves. There is a definite hierarchy in the colony. This is decided by various scent substances that the queen produces. The order is upset by the new queens, which produce different scents. Larvae and pupae are often carried from the nest. Many of the workers simply leave the nest.

When winter comes the nest is empty. The only survivors are the young fertilised queens, which have found themselves a good winter shelter. The old nest is not used again. Each year a new colony is built up from scratch.

When autumn comes and it gets colder, wasps become very aggressive. They attack each other. Here two wasps are fighting at the entrance to the nest.

The largest wasp in Western Europe is the hornet *(Vespa crabro)*. The workers can be up to 2.5 cm long. The queen can be over 3 cm long. The hornet lives, for the most part, in wooded areas. The nests are built in hollow trees. Occasionally nests are built in bird houses or even in the ground. Nests can be up to 40 cm × 50 cm large, depending on where they are built. Nests are built of rotting wood. The sting of the hornet is quite dangerous to humans.

The two most common wasps in Europe are the common wasp *(Vespula vulgaris)* and the German wasp *(Vespula germanica)*. The workers are about 1.5 cm long. The German wasp is a little larger and yellower than the common wasp. Except for the slight difference in size and colour, they are very similar in appearance and habits. Nests are often built in the ground, but are also built under eaves and in attics. You can recognise the nests by their mantles, which are made up of tiers laid like scales or roof tiles. These are very aggressive wasps and their sting is very uncomfortable. This is also true of the red wasp *(Vespula rufa)*. This wasp is found in damp and sandy areas. It is distinguished by the red forepart of its abdomen.

Other wasps are more harmless. They have a weaker poison. An example of this type is the tree wasp *(Dolichovespula sylvestris)*. This wasp often builds its nests hanging from tree branches or bushes. The covering of the nest is made of identical thin layers, fastened at the top.

Two types of wasps *(Pseudovespula osmissa and Pseudovespula austriaca)* have completely different habits from other wasps. They are parasites of the red wasp and the tree wasp. The queens emerge at a later

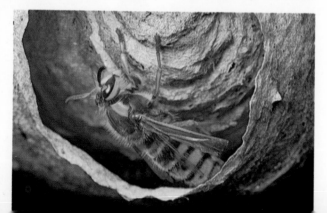

Queen at the entrance to her nest. To guard against the cold, the entrance has been moved to side of the nest. This shelters the nest from the wind.

stage than in other types of wasps. They find a nest be-
longing to the wasps of which they are parasites. Then
they sneak past the guards into the nest and kill the
queen. The alien queen lays her eggs in the cells. The
larvae are fed by the colony's workers. But the larvae
develop into new queens and males of the parasite type.
No workers are developed. After the original colony's
workers die, the nest breaks up.

Hanging wasps' nest in a white
hawthorn tree.

Some social wasps build nests that have no mantle. Their colonies are not as highly developed as those of other wasps. There is only one comb, and rarely more than 200 individuals in each nest. A colony can be started by various fertilised females. Only one of them will be queen. The others function as workers and do not lay eggs.

In addition to social wasps, there are also solitary wasps. Among these types there are females and males, but no workers. Females build simple nests. These have one or more cells, and are often built out of mud, in the shape of pots. These nests are found in the ground, in hollow plants, or on any suitable surface. In each cell the female lays an egg. Then she fills the cell with food

Two wasps meet. They use their antennae to find out whether they come from the same nest.

for the new larvae. The food consists for the most part of caterpillars that have been paralysed by poison from the female's sting. Finally the female closes the cell and does not return to it again. Even though in some areas one can find many nests of the same type, there is no cooperation between these wasps.

There are about 20 types of solitary wasps in Europe. The potter wasp is one of them. It is found in sandy heath areas, but is rare. It builds small elaborate pots of mud or clay mixed with grains of sand. These are attached to plant stems. The wasp fills up the pot with about ten caterpillars. Finally it lays an egg and seals the pot with clay.

Potter wasp. Its nest is shown above.

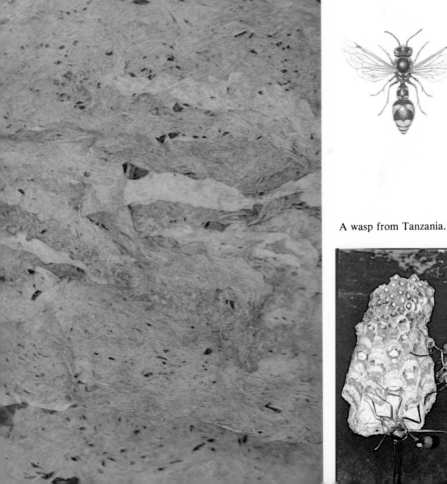

A wasp from Tanzania.

The sting

Wasp with protruding sting.

Wasps do not have many enemies. You can easily understand why if you have ever been stung by a wasp. Wasps use their stings to protect their colony against enemies. They attack objects that move. If you do not want to be stung it is best to stay still. You should not run away or try to hit them. Wasps seldom attack when they are out collecting food or building materials.

Both the queen and the workers can sting. The sting is in the tip of the abdomen. It has small barbs. These are not so strong that the sting remains in the wound. A wasp can sting more than once. When the sting penetrates the skin, it injects a poison into the wound. The poison contains various substances. These cause swelling and pain in the area around the wound. Some people are allergic to these substances. For these people it is very dangerous to be stung by a wasp. In some cases people can die from wasp stings.

If stung, you must wash the wound well to avoid infection. The wound should not be disturbed. The pain can be eased with an ice pack. If stung in the mouth, you should contact a doctor immediately.

Wasps can be very annoying if you want to eat outdoors in the summer. Try placing a glass with something sweet inside it some distance from where you are eating. The wasps may concentrate on this food instead of bothering you.

Garden spider with wasp.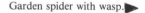

After a wasp sting.

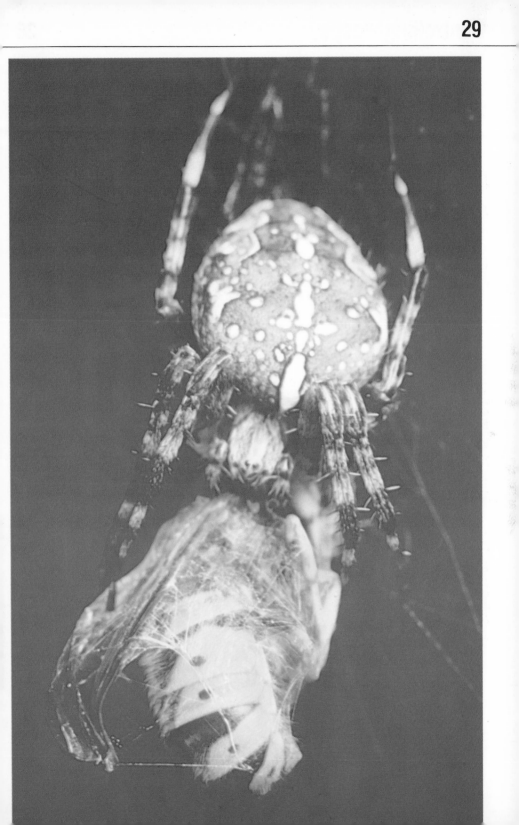

Wasps are both pests and useful insects. They are pests when they eat ripe fruit in orchards. This can mean quite a large loss for the fruit grower. They are also pests when they catch and kill honeybees and feed them to their larvae. Or when they steal honey from beehives.

It has been calculated that one type of wasp kills 33 honeybees per day, per wasp! It is obvious that if there are many thousand wasps in a nest, a beehive can be quickly overrun and emptied. Wasps can also carry disease, by carrying bacteria from refuse to people's food.

Wasps are useful insects when they catch flies. The inhabitants of a wasps' nest can eat many hundred flies a day. They also eat caterpillars, which otherwise do harm to various crops.

To control wasps, insecticides can be used. The best method is to sprinkle the entrance to the nest when it is dark. At that time of day all activity in the nest has ceased. This can be repeated a few times. After a few days the nest will be wiped out. To get rid of a nest in the ground, pour an anaesthetic into the nest and quickly cover up the entrance. The wasps will be stunned and die shortly afterwards from the poisonous fumes. If the nest is hanging, use cotton wool dipped in the poison. The cotton wool should be stuffed into the entrance hole.

There have been experiments to find other methods of controlling wasps, for example by feeding them sweets or meat containing insecticide. Since wasps feed each other, both adults and larvae spread the poison. But this method, as yet, has not given very good results.

In cake and fruit shops, where wasps can be a big problem, special light traps with ultraviolet light are

Wasps damage ripe fruit in orchards.

used. The wasps are attracted to the light. They are
sucked up by a ventilator into a wire basket. The trap
can contain a high voltage electric wire, which will kill
the wasps. Killing wasps with insecticide can indirectly
harm other animals. For example, a badger that has
eaten many poisoned wasps may also be poisoned.

Wasps on an apple.